# LETTERS TO A *Young*
# QUEEN

# LETTERS TO A *Young* QUEEN

## REDEFINING THEIR THRONE

JAY BARNETT

*Letters to a Young Queen*
©2015 by Jay Barnett
ISBN: 978-1505540949

Cover Design by Brandy Dallas
Cover model Jackie Goodwater
Text design by Lisa DeSpain of ebookconverting.com

# Contents

# Preface

American history is saturated with iconic women who have made a difference in society and a positive impact on women's rights. Throughout the 1900's women were granted several rights allowing them to have an equal voice in society—most notably the 19th amendment ratified in 1920, which granted women the right to vote. This milestone sparked a societal change that elevated the place of women. Women of the 1900's were fortunate to have so many fearless leaders and trailblazers to admire and respect—Amelia Earhart, Helen Keller, Rosa Parks and Eleanor Roosevelt, to name a few. Their tireless efforts inspired younger women to become agents of change and move beyond the barriers set forth. More importantly, many young women were raised with manners, taught proper etiquette and instilled with confidence—behaviors and qualities indicative of a young Queen. These solid upbringings, coupled with the great examples set by iconic role models, resulted in women reaching greater heights in what was once deemed "a man's world." Women shattered the glass ceiling—landing positions in traditionally male-dominated industries such as politics, banking and science.

Despite this progression, there exist several prominent female figures in our current culture who detract from the inroads made thus far. The twenty-first century brought with it a drastic shift in the type of female leaders whom young women idolize. The days of positive female role models have slowly disappeared as reality stars and entertainers dominate the attention of our young girls. Young women of this generation have lost sight of the numerous sacrifices made to ensure and protect their freedoms and rights. The path that we tread as a society begs to ask, what will we reflect on in the next decade? How do we stop a perpetual cycle of uneducated behaviors carried out by our young women? How do we extinguish their foolish acts plaguing our society and resembling anything but a Queen?

I've had the privilege and opportunity to work with many young girls through the Women of Excellence Project, a program dedicated to the mentoring and mental development of young girls. Throughout my work, I began to witness a recurring pattern associated with young girls—the need for acceptance and validation. More importantly, I discovered that they seemed more open to advice and guidance from an adult male, and I quickly realized I had something to offer. The more I remained consistently free of judgment, the more open and honest they became toward my thoughts and ideas. Even at an early age, these girls wish to pursue what is socially accepted. If provocative dancing and posting racy pictures on social media are socially acceptable, then they will subscribe to these trends. If idolizing reality stars famous for lewd and inappropriate behavior is the norm instead of looking up to prominent historical figures known for effecting positive change in society, then that is what will capture their attention. It is now our responsibility to change their mindset.

*Letters to a Young Queen* is a collection of letters stemming from my personal experiences and thoughts specifically geared toward young girls. The book highlights the struggles and triumphs of young women I've encountered through the WE Project. *Letters to a Young Queen* is for the fatherless little girl desperately seeking male attention and craving the encouragement, discipline and authority that only a father figure can provide. These letters will inspire and empower young girls from all backgrounds to grow into the Queens they are destined to become.

# You Are a Queen

*Dear Queen,*

What is a Queen? A Queen is a ruler and monarch with the power to make all the decisions in her kingdom, which can be shared with her King. Every person has the capability to rule over a kingdom with his or her family. What is a kingdom? A kingdom consists of your mind, body and soul. As a ruler, you possess the power to make all decisions in your life. It is crucial to keep in mind that with each choice you make, you are making it as a Queen. Knowing who you are allows you to be more powerful. Knowing that you are a Queen changes the dynamics of how you rule your kingdom. Many

*Keep in mind that with each choice you make, you are making it as a Queen.*

of our young girls simply don't have the full knowledge or understanding of who they are and, in turn, become what they see. If our young women don't see other women displaying self-control, self-awareness and self-worth, how can they learn to correctly emulate these characteristics? Realistically, young girls have more power than they understand. *All* young girls are Queens, despite their circumstance or environment. A Queen cannot choose her parents or how her life journey began. However, she has the ability to choose how her life journey will continue. Most of what you will learn in this life will not come from a classroom. Rather, life itself will act as your teacher. No matter what you have been told by your family, friends or peers, always remember *you are a Queen*. By choosing the habits and behaviors of royalty, you allow the Queen who resides in you to spring forth to life. Music, peers and especially men cannot bring your inner Queen to life. I pray this letter empowers you to define yourself as the Queen who you were born to be. I want you to redefine your throne by

*Your mind is your kingdom and you must protect it at all costs.*

challenging the way you think and how you view yourself. Your mind is your kingdom and you must protect it at all costs. Cherish it as if your life depends on it. Be aware of the naysayers who seek to deter you from sitting on your rightful throne. Stay away from those who choose not to carry themselves as royalty. A true Queen surrounds herself with like-minded individuals. Every morning when you wake up, put on your invisible crown and wear it with pride, dignity and excellence. Smile for no reason, laugh at nothing and give compliments simply for the sake of complimenting.

I use QUEEN as an acronym to speak into the lives of young girls all over the world. You are **Q**uality that exceeds any materialistic item. You are priceless. The world needs your input. You are **Unique** and there will never be another you. You don't have to compete with anyone but yourself. Always **Educate** yourself as this will empower you to be your best. No matter where you are, always use proper **Etiquette** and conduct yourself as royalty. Regardless of any circumstance or situation you may be in, **Never** remove your crown. The mere fact that you can recognize who you are as a Queen makes a statement far beyond anything you can ever verbalize.

*You Are a Queen*

*King Jay*

# Beautiful Butterfly

*A Poem by Jay Barnett*

You were born and shaped into a world of sin

But on the bright side,
you were equipped with the power to win

You are no longer a caterpillar;
you have changed and emerged from within.

Spread your beautiful wings and
ascend into the clouds

Don't look back at yesterday,
today is a new day and you should be proud

Fly above the mountains,
scream your freedom and be loud,

If no one else tells you, I am so very proud.

You were born to be great,
your purpose and success await

But it is up to you to not keep them waiting,
so don't be late.

While others fly and chase behind goons,

Just remember the galaxy waits for a woman's
footprints to touch the moon.

Many started on the journey of
breaking from the cocoon,

Somehow they lost their way,
because they left too soon.

They didn't realize the need to learn how to fly;
it helps to prepare you for the struggle,

That way you know how to search for the right advice
when you find yourself in trouble.

The mirror reflects the outer,
but your character reflects your inner

There is no need to change, so stop complaining
about how you want to be thinner

You are a beautiful butterfly that is born a winner.

Remember this: Never stop flying for someone who
can't win with you

Your journey is unlike any other,
if they can't handle it, I guess they can't fly with you

Your wings are bright
because you were meant to be seen

Just be careful where you land, beautiful butterfly,
all leaves are not green

I would hate for you to get contaminated
and become bitter and mean.

Fly with other butterflies that compliment you

Make sure to distance yourself
from those who aren't true

Real friendships reflect commitment
and nothing but the truth.

Beautiful butterfly, make sure to keep smiling
every day of the week

Always surround yourself with peace
and those who desire to live in harmony

Beautiful butterfly,
you don't have to be drunk to be in love

Remain sober so you can enjoy the heights of your
success when you are flying above

Every now and then, reach out to another
even with just a simple hug

We live in a society where women don't realize
they are so precious

So many spend a lot of their time chasing the wind,
only to be left feeling deserted and useless

If only they remembered the day they entered into
the world, already crowned as princesses

So appreciate the beauty of your cocoon,
the colors of your wings and forget about the rest

Life is about who you are becoming
and not about what you get

One day you will have to answer
if you gave it your best

Always remember, the world is huge
and there is enough room in the friendly skies

For all of you to fly free as beautiful butterflies.

# Two Way Mirror

Dear Queen,

I hope this letter lifts your spirit and builds you internally, which in turn will change what you perceive externally. The mirror can be very discouraging depending on how you see yourself. Sometimes the reflection is not what we desire because we see a different picture than what is cast. Our society has transformed into a very superficial environment where beauty is based on the outer surface rather than the inner being. It can be difficult to accept what the mirror reflects, but what you see is not up to the mirror. Queen, it is up to *you* to accept what you see. Do not foolishly and swiftly give that power to others. The mirror is capable of displaying one image. Is it the same image that you see and appreciate? No one will accept what you don't appreciate. Until you appreciate what you see, it will be impossible to accept yourself. I understand the pressures you receive from your peers and from those around you, but your mirror hangs on your wall, not theirs. Don't compare your mirror with anyone else's. Your mirror only reflects the uniqueness you possess. Looking into someone else's mirror is akin to committing a crime against yourself. Do not incriminate yourself by using someone else's perception. A filter on your photo won't enhance what you

*It is not about covering up your imperfections— it is about looking past them and still seeing the beauty.*

don't already see. Queen, it is your responsibility to clean your mirror with positive affirmations and re-inforcement. I am reminded of a young mentee of mine, who I will call Sara. Sara was a beautiful girl with the brains to follow. However, she struggled to find herself because of her comparisons to friends who were curvier or thinner. I remember asking her what she saw when she

looked in the mirror. She said she didn't like her reflection. I wasn't sure at which mirror she was looking. The girl I saw was very beautiful so I couldn't comprehend what she was seeing. She talked about the pursuit of perfection. I explained to her that it is simply unattainable. No one is perfect. Airbrushing and makeup only hide so much. Finding your beauty is not about covering up your imperfections—it is about looking past them and still seeing the beauty present within you. Queen, there will *never* be another you. You're an original who cannot be duplicated. Using filters on photos these days has tarnished authentic images. Everyone wants the perfect picture, but there can be no such thing. You are the picture God made—fearfully and wonderfully. Therefore, you are picture perfect because He is a perfect God. Don't let society change what you see in your mirror, because you are responsible for your own reflection. People will receive you how they perceive you, so be careful what your reflection gives off. If your father wasn't there to affirm you or validate your beauty, that's okay. I am encouraging you to keep seeing that beautiful reflection in the mirror. When the past rears its ugly head in your mirror, keep in mind that it is out of focus, existing only in the background. However, your image and beauty continue to be in the forefront of your reflection. Even if you were violated by someone you trusted, keep seeing your beauty. Don't let past experience change your present reflection. You are a Queen who is equipped with great gifts and talents. The world is in need of your input and contributions. There will be times when you will have to be on the outside looking in because the outside will change. Always look deep into who you really are. Search beneath the surface to find your true quality. Changing the exterior won't matter if you don't change the interior. Many hide behind the lipstick, blush and mascara because they are afraid to accept themselves as they are. Instead, they spend their lives trying to be someone they saw in someone else's mirror. Don't be

*You are a Queen who is equipped with great gifts and talents. The world is in need of your input and contributions.*

so concerned with how you measure up that you miss out on being yourself. When it comes to males, make sure you seek out those who genuinely appreciate you rather than compare you to a model. You can't be yourself while attempting to be someone else. Not every person can be a supermodel or a size 2. No matter what social media displays, it isn't reality. Pay closer attention to pictures, as they don't always reveal the reality and truth of a person. Perception is everything. The world wouldn't be real if everyone were the same. In closing, discover your abilities, gifts and strengths by paying attention to your mirror. Change your perspective by looking beyond the reflection of what you see and discovering who you are inside. You control the two way mirror by seeing what you see and what the mirror reflects. I see a beautiful Queen who is destined to rule her kingdom by seeing herself as a QUEEN.

Who do you see?

*Keep Ruling*
*King Jay*

# Attitude

*Dear Queen,*

I hope this letter encourages you to have a positive attitude toward yourself and life in general. Your attitude is truly everything. You are perceived, judged and critiqued by everyone you meet and interact with based on your attitude and how you come across, both positively and negatively. Whether you portray a positive or negative attitude depends entirely on you. You may feel that you have a right to elicit a negative attitude because of your circumstance. You may feel that life has been crappy to you, so why should you have a positive outlook on life? My response to you is, why not? Even the most extreme and dire circumstances can reap positive results. It all comes down to perspective and how you handle it. A positive attitude in any situation will yield positive results, just as a negative one will give negative results. Your response to any situation is completely in your control. A negative situation does not automatically entitle you to a negative attitude. You owe it to yourself to remain positive, as hard as it may be at times. A bad attitude make a beautiful woman very unattractive. No

LETTERS TO A YOUNG QUEEN

one likes negativity or wants to be around it. A bad attitude is a contagious disease. Its infectious nature causes it to spread quickly. The only way to stop it or slow it down is to maintain a good attitude and approach situations prepared to maintain control. Sowing your surroundings with positivity will reap positivity in life.

Queen, you don't need a bad attitude to be noticed or recognized. Being mean and hateful does not guarantee you the respect you may crave. There are very few rulers who have *successfully* ruled their kingdom with bad attitudes. Sure, it may have helped them out on the battlefield, but did their people adore them? Would their people voluntarily rally behind them if they had any other choice? As a Queen, your attitude should be a display of the main principle that you live by, which is royalty. Always carry yourself as royalty. Always remember the saying, "Your attitude determines your aptitude." Queen, having the right attitude affects your ability to learn and comprehend. How can you learn if you have a negative attitude toward everyone and everything? Don't hinder yourself from growing into the Queen you were chosen to become. You cannot control anyone else's attitude but your own. You are in charge of your behavior toward your family, friends and everyone around you. It can be difficult to overlook past situations but you must be the bigger person. Being the bigger person ultimately adds more value to your life. Always think beyond your current situation. Tomorrow always comes and brings with it judgment from the attitude you display today. It may not seem fair, but life is not fair. People will judge you by how they remember you. Give them something positive on which to reflect. Being loud, mean, ratchet and angry all the time is simply not cute. No matter how much makeup is applied, it will not hide the blemishes of a bad attitude. Whatever you may be dealing with, always try to look on the bright side. Yes, the bright side exists when you change your attitude toward your present situations. Think about the good in bad situations. See the best in others even when they look to expose the worst in you. Maintain a good attitude. To quote John Maxwell, "It is easier to maintain a good attitude than to regain a good attitude." Think about that for a second. Once you respond negatively, it leaves a lasting impression on people. Perception *is* reality. Instead of losing your cool, keep it.

A Queen never comes off her throne to engage in meaningless acts. Don't go left; go right. Don't blast people on social media and send subliminal messages to express your anger. Display and keep having a good attitude in all aspects of life. With the power of social networking, nothing goes unnoticed today, so be aware of your actions. Don't create a permanent result based on a temporary

*Don't create a permanent result based on a temporary problem. Think, Queen.*

problem. *Think*, Queen. Surround yourself with people who have a good attitude toward life, school and their situations. I noticed many girls I mentored had bad attitudes simply so they could fit in with other friends who also had bad attitudes. Never let your feelings be affected by someone else's situation, because you will reap the consequences of their actions. Bad company will corrupt good character. Whether you know it or not, your attitude introduces you before you ever do.

In conclusion, I don't know what your current situation is, Queen. However, your attitude will determine the outcome, whether positive or negative. Maintain a great *royalitude*:

being respectful and positive toward situations concerning others. I created that word just for you, Queen. I know your reality may be too negative for you to be positive, but know that someone else always has it worse. Always think of others and not just yourself. Make an effort to reach out to another young Queen. We all have our problems but we can accomplish so much more with good attitudes. If we could all have great and positive attitudes, it would shift the atmosphere so all mankind can respect one another. You need to step up and be the one who makes a difference. Queen, one person with a good attitude can change a room full of people. Why shouldn't that person be you?

*King Jay*

# Little Girl

*A Poem by Jay Barnett*

Somewhere in front of a mirror stands a little girl,
and all she sees is the ugliest person in the world.

I want to tell her that God shaped her like a diamond
and He protects her like she is His precious pearl.

But unfortunately, she will mostly be judged
by the exterior,

Without taking the time to search
beneath the surface.

Little girl, when God made you, He had a purpose.

You don't have to search any longer,
because everything you need is inside.

You have value. There is no reason to hide.

Always hold your head up and
never lose your sense of pride.

You are a beautiful rose that is ready to bloom,

But be careful of those who pressure you
to blossom too soon.

Here is a piece of advice: Never chase boys,
friends or things,

Create your own lane and chase your own dreams.

The truth of the matter is,
certain perceptions are never what they seem.

And, to be brutally honest,
some girls and women are really mean.

But you, you're different, because you are a Queen.

Stay seated on your throne so that when that day
comes, your King knows exactly where to find you.

There is no greater joy than to be
dancing with your ring, instead of BANDS.

Seriously, these boys can't even describe to you
what makes a real MAN.

You see, society tells you to wear a disguise, but for
what reason would you want to live a lie?

You possess the powers to be
the woman you want to be.

So stop saying that you are giving it a TRY.

As for true love, it can only be found in God and it
can only be shared with the man who pursues Him.

Don't sell your soul for a steak dinner with shrimp,

Because if you're not up on game,
you will find yourself getting pimped.

These dudes are out here lurking,

They will have you all on Facebook and Instagram
straight twerking.

5 years later, 3 kids, now you are working for cash.

Little girl, if you don't want to be associated with
garbage, don't carry yourself like trash.

Carry yourself like a Woman of Excellence and keep
yourself in a higher class.

I am not trying to be your father,
I'm just kicking knowledge.

At this point in your life, you should be
preparing for college,

Not in a bed, building mileage.

Some of these dudes are really trying to live out
what they hear on these tracks,

Just know that you are worth more than
lying down on your back.

Little girl, you have to be careful of what you
let get in your head,

Contrary to what you may have heard, your value
can't be determined by what you do in bed.

Be smart and intelligent,
or else you will end up on meds.

Be yourself, stop listening to all of these "Simon Says."

Get a dream and create a vision board,
because that's how you get ahead.

Little girl, there will never be another you.
So be who you are,

Stop floating in the galaxy and
shine bright like a star.

Always hold your standards high,
so you don't depreciate like an old car.

As far as my eyes can see, little girl, your future
looks bright thus far.

I want to encourage you to keep ruling your territory.

You don't have to wait on some guy acting like
Miguel talking about how he adores you,

Because one day the right friend, the right man, will
come along and truly appreciate your story.

No matter what happens, always stand your ground,

Get in the ring of life and go round for round.

And never argue with your critics,

Because a Queen never removes her crown.

Keep Ruling, Little Girl

# Love Thyself

*Dear Queen,*

I hope this letter empowers you to love yourself beyond what has been projected upon you. "Love" is such a powerful word, but unfortunately, it is used so casually in this generation. There is very little thought put into its use. I want you to really grasp the reality that it is only when you truly love yourself that you are truly able to love another. Too many of our young Queens give their bodies with the expectation of receiving love in return. This will only lead to heartache. From the bottom of my heart, I hope this letter changes your perception and view on love. Not just from the perspective of a man, but from the heart of a King who desires to see you love yourself first before pursuing to fulfill the absence of love.

What is love? To me, God is love. According to *Webster's Dictionary,* one definition of "love" describes it as affection based on admiration. Although there are several definitions, this one resonates with me more than the others. The word is a noun in the dictionary but becomes a verb when used in a different context. Think about it: If you don't take the time to admire something or someone first, how can you expect to have affection toward that thing or person? Society, pop culture and broken homes have been the reasons many of our young girls don't admire themselves, which in turn makes it hard for them to have affection or love toward themselves. I want to challenge you, Queen. It is not your fault if you did not receive love, but it *is* your responsibility to love yourself nonetheless. When you change how you think, you also change how you view everything. We live in a society of fatherless daughters, and it has become the norm for a young girl to create her own definition of love rather than receive and observe it correctly in a loving and supporting environment. When a warped perspective becomes the sole source of reasoning, one can

*You are important, and it is vital that you love yourself. Only you can repair your broken heart.*

end up in less than ideal situations. Many young girls have decided that giving their bodies is love, but it is a life-altering decision. Sex is not love, Queen; sex is an expression of love intended for marriage. Do not allow your environment to force you into thinking that love is all about giving up something. Love, however, does require something of you. It starts with you. Love yourself and learn to be happy with yourself before you

can expect anyone else to love you. Invest in yourself. That is the greatest expression of admiration. Love yourself even if your father is not involved in your life or didn't display love toward you. A young mentee once said to me, "My dad broke my heart long before any dude had a chance to." There are many of you who feel the same way, and I empathize with you.

However, you are important, and it is vital that you love yourself. It doesn't matter if your heart has been broken—it is up to you to mend it. Only you can repair your broken heart. You will wait a lifetime outside a repair shop that will never open if you depend on someone else to fix your heart. Therefore, Queen, the responsibility belongs to you. I understand that not receiving love makes it hard to give it at times, but you owe love to yourself. I know you may feel alone and lost with no one to care about at times, and it may seem that everyone has cast you off to the side. Beautiful Queen, love yourself, even if it hurts. A man or a boy won't value what you don't value. You must love and value yourself first. It is by choice that you love yourself beyond your circumstances. Admire yourself; don't wait on friends or people to do it. Never wait for the approval of others. Otherwise, you will always be searching for acceptance. Many women who never learned to first love themselves are now dealing with the consequences. They are plagued with self-doubt, pity, insecurities and an overall lack of confidence. There are so many unfortunate consequences of living a life without loving yourself first, including having a child out of wedlock, getting sent to prison or living with a life-altering or even life-ending disease. Do not neglect yourself. Queen, it is only through loving yourself that you allow yourself the advantage of being exempt from less-than-stellar consequences. When you start to love yourself, your decision-making abilities will dramatically improve for the better. I promise you they will. This will redirect your thought process to prioritize you and your needs. If a guy only says he loves you when you are undressed, *think*! Ask yourself why you have to give up something in order to receive a false representation of love. You don't have to give up anything. I am encouraging you to give to yourself first. It doesn't matter how many boys or men you have at your feet. If you don't put yourself first and foremost, it will only create a bigger hole in your life. You are searching for something you never had and are expecting someone to do what you never did—simply loving yourself. I know that you want to feel accepted, appreciated and valued. We all do. All humans want those feelings, but there comes a responsibility from desiring them. We must take accountability for doing for ourselves what we want others to do for us.

If they don't like you, love yourself. If they don't think you're cool enough, love yourself. If you feel you're not beautiful, I am telling you that you are. Love yourself. If your mother has never embraced you, love yourself. You may not know your father, but there is a father who will always love you. His name is God and He says, love yourself. You must provide yourself with the affection you desire. Until you love and appreciate yourself, no one will, so remember you have a responsibility. Keep your body for your King; don't give it up for false love. If a man can't respect your choice, then he is not the guy with whom you want to be involved. And if he replies that he will go somewhere else, let him go, and tell him that you love yourself too much to exchange it for nothing. When our young Queens start loving themselves, it will change the lyrics in the songs that we hear today. Why not start with loving yourself today? Smile and hold your head up. Even if you are fatherless and regardless of where you reside, the inner city, suburbs or country, love yourself. Never place the responsibility you owe yourself in the hands of others. Continue loving yourself, Queen. Always.

Repeat these words:

Today I will admire myself with positive thoughts and words that uplift me to be a Queen. I will do unto myself what I expect from others. I will love who I am, who I was and who I am becoming. My love toward myself is not determined by music, statistics, stereotypes, my past, my environment or what I don't have. I will love myself beyond my disappointment, my hurt, my pain and my failures. God loves me, and so do I. Today, I will love myself because I am a QUEEN.

King Jay

# *Emotions*

*Dear Queen,*

It is my hope for you that this letter touches your heart and ignites a change in you to be the Queen you were destined to be. I want to take a moment and write to you about the effects of not being in control of your emotions. No matter what is happening in your world, it is of the utmost importance that you always maintain your composure and never let the negativity that may surround you break you down. Acting out in anger, sadness, rage or any other sort of powerful emotion typically begets a negative outcome. Our society's appetite for drama and chaos is steadily growing. The increase in reality television, where it has become the norm for women to insert themselves in confrontations and hostile environments, attracts more viewers daily. It seems as if acting strictly based

*Acting out in anger, sadness, rage or any other sort of powerful emotion typically begets a negative outcome.*

on emotions has become an expected and accepted part of our culture. This sort of behavior has now crossed over into the real world and we are seeing countless videos of it popping up on the Internet, waiting to go viral. Young Queens are fighting each other for no apparent reason other than to get famous. This type of behavior will only continue to influence our younger generation to post videos of fights, arguments and other malicious acts all for the same misguided aspiration.

It seems that a lot of young girls are angry at their current situations. Anger that is channeled incorrectly is a disaster waiting to happen. You may not like your home, school or classmates, but your future depends on your present choices, regardless of your current circumstances. I often think back to a young mentee who was always in a confrontation with someone. The smallest thing would set her off and she would be ready to fight. I would often challenge her to not let her emotions overtake her, but she liked being angry. She said she felt good when she fought. I could relate because I recalled the anger I felt in my teenage years when I experienced the divorce of my parents. I had a short fuse. I would always get kicked out of class. I eagerly awaited confrontations and often provoked people to say something just so I had an excuse to fight. Looking back, I realize that I was looking for someone to pay attention to me, just as many of you young Queens are looking for attention from things and people. We feel good after we fight because we feel validated. In some way, we feel we have been hurt or wronged. And in turn, we want to inflict vengeance on the nearest victim. I completely understand. However, Queen, I want this letter to challenge you to learn how to gain control of your emotions. It is considered abnormal nowadays to be the peaceful one who walks away. The pressure to react has intensified, especially since everyone has cell phones out and ready to film. Queen, even in your angriest moments, you must remain in control of your emotions and not let peer pressure make decisions for you, because it is you who will have to suffer the consequences. When you understand what it means to be in control of your emotions, you will have the power to redirect those emotions in a positive way. But it is up to you. Queen, people are going to upset you. They are going to say something about your makeup, hair, shoes and other things that do not reflect your true character. Become

*Even in your angriest moments, you must remain in control of your emotions.*

numb to the negative words and actions of other people. Not everyone is your friend. Are you being honest with yourself when you consider every person you come across a friend? No matter what you do or say, there will be someone who won't be happy or like you. More often than not, he or she won't have a reason. If that's the case, resolving the issue using raw emotion won't guarantee you a positive outcome but likely will lead to a regretful one.

Queen, your emotions can guide you astray because they cause you to act without thinking. There is a reason for the tried-and-true saying, "Use your head, not your heart." Always think before you react. Too many of us didn't think before acting and are now paying the consequences. I am reminded of a young lady I worked with, whom we can call Tara. She acted based on her emotions, which cost her dearly. Tara had gotten in trouble at school. When she arrived home, her mother walked in to her room to confront her. As her mother approached, Tara became enraged and grabbed her mother. She began pushing her toward the wall. Tara was much larger than her mother. Tara's rage grew stronger as her emotions rushed to the surface. She wrapped her hands around her mother's neck and didn't let go. It wasn't until her mother stopped fighting back that Tara finally let go. Her mother's body collapsed and lay lifeless on the floor. Tara stood in shock, not believing what had just occurred. Uncontrollable emotions took Tara to a level of rage she never felt before in just a matter of seconds. I can personally rest assured knowing that she was not intentionally trying to harm her mother that day. When we don't control our emotions, they can take us to a place of no return.

As a young female, you are more naturally inclined to be more emotional than your male counterpart. This is a beautiful thing, as it is what makes you who you are. As beautiful as it is, it can be just as equally dangerous. You have to take back the power of your emotions. Queen, you have too much to lose, and when you realize this, it will change the decisions you make. Don't risk your future for a short-lived fame or temporary satisfaction that may cost you a lifetime of misery. Never give up your crown or lose your kingdom over emotional reactions.

*Don't jeopardize your life for the sake of feelings that will eventually pass.*

Don't jeopardize your life for the sake of feelings that will eventually pass. Let them talk about you. Who cares? Let them laugh. Who cares? You must know that you are worth more than the satisfaction of living up to the stereotypes that society has in place for you. So many young Queens are dying and going to jail because they don't restrain their anger. Start today by taking control of your emotions and choosing your actions in the heat of the moment. Someone will try you, but maintain your cool, Queen. Bear in mind that controlling your emotions does not mean you should suppress them. This can be equally if not more dangerous, like a volcano waiting to erupt, as it did with Tara. It is crucial to find a healthy outlet to release emotions. Prayer, exercise, meditation, counseling and finding a supportive friend or mentor are all great ways to help you channel and release your emotions.

Repeat this:

"I am a Queen. I will not be negatively influenced by anything or anyone around me. I am responsible for my emotions and actions and, therefore, I now take back the power to control them."

*Keep Ruling*

*King Jay*

# Violated

A Poem by Jay Barnett
*Inspired by: Anonymous*

Unprotected by family and loved ones

Who knew they would violate me and
now I feel like I weigh a ton

Touched in the wrong places

By people I knew and now I
can't look them in their faces

Sometimes I wish I could stop because it's not
worth finishing this race

It started as innocent at first
but then he became very bold

I ask myself, how can I get married?
This monster has a piece of my soul

I feel empty because I can never be whole

Yes, I was violated

He told me I was beautiful and pretty

How could he mess up his mind to take advantage
of little ol' me?

Mom thought I was lying, but now she sees

Yes, it was family who did this to me


Yes, I was violated

I am one in every 3 girls who was molested

The people who do these things are possessed

It's hard for me to look in the mirror
because at times I don't feel my best

But today is a new day, I will get up, get dressed
and demand my respect


Yes, I was violated

It has been hard to leave my past behind

I replay it over and over and over in my mind

But I must open my eyes to the present
before my future goes blind

God heals and so does time


Yes, I was violated

I want to speak to all the women
who have been violated

I want to encourage them to be bold
and to not be intimidated

We may be victims but we have the victory

Because they may have taken our bodies
but they didn't take our dignity

Therefore we are vindicated by our own liberty

Walk tall and hold your head high


Yes, we were violated

Life is one big classroom and we will graduate

Beyond the hurt and pain

Walk where there is no path and
create your own lane

As eagles, let's fly above the storm and the rain

You are royalty so always stand your ground

Stay in the ring of life and fight round for round

And continue to strut with your invisible crown


Violated, but I made it

# Intelligence

Dear Queen,

I hope this letter empowers you to educate yourself beyond the classroom and influences you to be the best in every situation you encounter. I hope you discover your hidden treasure of intelligence and maximize it to its full potential. Dressing for success at school used to be a privilege on Career Day. Both the boys and the girls wore business suits, looking like bosses. Nowadays, bosses come in all shapes, forms and outfits, and the appreciation for dressing for success has faded. This is the era of the "bad chick." Unfortunately, this label has nothing to do with the potential of a young girl's mind and everything to do with her body's shape and movements. The value of preparing for success through education has taken a backseat to the chick who strips or the model who floods timelines with her bathroom photo shoots. It doesn't matter if she can't do basic math. She ranks high because of what she can do with her body. What has our society come to? We care more about the performance of a woman's body than her mind. Music helps depict the sexism that grabs the attention of our young girls. It paints the illusion that outer beauty pays more than a degree from a respected institution. Social media and music bombard young girls with the bad chick image so much so that they start to pursue this illusion. It aches my heart to see young women chase this empty image with its empty promises. Queen, I wish you could see more positive role models, both male and female. I hope that one day there will be more entertainers you can proudly aspire to be. It is sad that social media didn't boast about a young teen named Eesha Khare, who created a supercapacitor prototype charger that charges within 20–30 seconds.

*The music industry paints the illusion that outer beauty pays more than a degree from a respected institution.*

It's disheartening that Thessalonika Arzu-Embry didn't receive more publicity for completing her bachelor's degree in psychology at Chicago State University at the age of 14. The Oscars were graced by the presence of an amazing young girl who gave a breathtaking performance in her Hollywood debut, but did you know that Lupita Nyong'o received her master's degree from the Yale School of Drama? Either way, I am sure you're up-to-date on the most recent girl fight since social media inundates newsfeeds with that type of news by the minute.

Queen, I want you to know that being intelligent is the new bad chick. One day your body won't be able to answer the questions of life, and you will have to articulate your philosophy intellectually. Your response will be determined by what you have fed your mind. I am challenging you to be more than what you see and hear. It doesn't take a lot of intelligence to press the send button or comment with your opinion. Expand your capacity for learning; grow in more than one area. Being fashionable is great, but have you tapped into your other talents beyond the belts, boots and earrings? What do you bring to society? The dropout rate is increasing among teen girls daily, the primary cause being teenage pregnancy. The second is low self-esteem stemming from an inability to learn, which leads to young women quitting school. This epidemic has led to our young Queens pursuing stripping as their career. They feel they can make more money in one night than in a 40-hour work week. This may be true, but Queen, you have more to offer than making your body a business. Eventually, your body will go out of business. It is hard to desire that which you have not been inspired by or have seen exemplified. Contrary to what you may have seen or heard, twerking is not a talent. Being called a "bad bitch" should not be the highlight of your existence. Being intelligent is attractive far beyond the surface, because your mind holds the key to unlock doors for your talents. If you are only feeding the physical aspect and giving no attention to your mental one, you will one day find yourself on the outside looking in. Your education and your intelligence will take you places your face

*Being intelligent is attractive far beyond the surface, because your mind holds the key to your talents.*

can't. I am speaking to the beautiful intelligent Queen who is inside. I am placing a demand that you revive that part of you. Be different, embrace being smart and enjoy discovering the bright person you are. Don't be a victim of this corrupt fantasy that beauty pays. A true Queen understands that her beauty is a byproduct of her existence because her decisions are made with her mind. As a positive male figure, I encourage you to be smart and make wise decisions. Rule your kingdom with clever moves that will reflect your beautiful mind. Be the kind of woman who makes other women want to look up to you. Every morning when you wake up, look in the mirror and say, "I am more than a face. I am more than a body. I am intelligent. I am purpose-driven. I am valuable. I am not a bad chick. *I am a Queen.*"

*King Jay*

# First Things First

*A Poem by Jay Barnett*

I think beauty is overrated,
check your label because a pretty face
will soon be outdated.
Dudes used to rock platinum,
but now they switch it to gold but it's plated.
You gave it up on the first night, 9 months later,
don't you wish you would have waited?
Sometimes you have to take a step back and
get your thoughts situated.
Don't be defined by your circumstances.
I think it's time to turn your tassel
now that you've graduated.

Broken smile behind your lipstick and
tears behind the eye shadow hide
what is really making you sick.
Uncontrolled emotions will have you with MIX,
mixed feelings like a jelly donut with no filling
and only God can provide you healing.

Open your eyes and see the truth,
while he was doing you,
he was someone else, boo.
It's not funny when the game is over,
and the score is "YOU LOSE."
Now what do you do?

Baby girl, cherish your heart and
stop selling your feelings like used car parts.
Be careful of the illusion of lust,
because once you touch,
you will learn it is too much to handle.
Now you are Olivia Pope because you are
in a scandal, and once you have that soul tie,
it's hard to untangle.
Remember what God said:
Your body is a temple,
so stop letting these men get a sample.

I'm No T.D. Jakes, but I want to teach, not preach.
Pass the collection plate,
because it's time that you learn a new way to speak.
You are your words,
and your words are a part of your speech.
No shade thrown, but please have several seats.
When you come to the table,
please be able to do more than just eat.

Jesus, take the wheel.
Where is the woman who is beautiful and meek?
Ladies, discover your purpose
instead of criticizing what is on someone's feet.

It is hard to dance to your own music
when you can't even create your own beat.
Be careful of what your eyes see,
because the best things in life are not free.
You are priceless. Wouldn't you agree?

Be different and take a stand.
Never trust a man who doesn't have God in his plan.
Last but not least, marry yourself,
before you date a MAN.

# Your Body

Dear Queen,

> "He who gains a victory over other men is strong, but he
> who gains a victory over himself is all-powerful."
>
> —Lao Tzu

This quote from Lao Tzu is one of the most powerful statements I have ever heard. It asserts that when you gain control over yourself, you become powerful beyond your imagination. Many of the challenges we face today arise from a lack of self-control. Money, sex and power can destroy a person if he or she lacks discipline and self-control. In this letter, I challenge you, Queen, to understand that your body is your temple and that you must develop self-control in order to rule your kingdom. I hope you unearth the value within you so that you can live a healthy and rewarding life.

Planned Parenthood conducted a study stating that 2,000 teenage girls get pregnant every day in the United States. The study also revealed that 7 out of 10 teens are sexually active, even more so than their parents. With numbers this high, the risk of STDs, HIV and other health issues increases substantially. In addition, the value of the female body has declined. Stripping and modeling are sought-after careers because they pursue money and fame. It's also common to see half-naked females all over social networks. The desire for attention is dramatically increasing, especially because of our acceptance of the "anything goes" mentality, more commonly referred to as "the thirst is real." Our young girls believe that the more they expose and do with their bodies, the more attention they'll receive. This type of attention is self-destructive and can lead to teenage pregnancy or disease. However, what if you realized that your health is more valuable than temporary satisfaction? Would you still engage in risky sexual behavior? I have heard many devastating stories from young mentees that will make anyone cry. It hurts to know that self-respect is becoming a rarity. Access to social media can corrupt many young women if they don't practice self-control or know their worth. You can upload pictures instantly and capture every moment of your life with the click of a button. Taking selfies has become part of the daily regimen for many females. Timelines are exploding with photos of young girls piling on makeup, posing with duck faces and, the most popular, exposing their rear ends in mirrors. Our young girls are going to extremes to receive attention. Queen, these behaviors have increased the appetite of boys lurking on social networks. They flood these types of photos with "likes," comments and responses that feed the vulnerable at heart. Queen, it is important that you maintain will power and self-control despite the comments. It is easy to fall victim to this false sense of validation when you aren't receiving positive affirmation from a father or a male figure. Even with a present father, you are not wholly exempt because guys will attempt to say all the things that you seek to hear. You must stand your ground in your kingdom of mind, body and soul, because once you exchange your body for attention, you devalue yourself. Be conscious of the devices that are in place for you to become a negative statis-tic. Don't exchange your physical body for an emotional attachment that could plague you forever. Value your body, Queen. If you have to lie down in order to feel love, then it is not love. It is a false representation of love. Your body is a temple. Don't allow a man to use you as an object at his whim. You are precious, Queen, and your body should be preserved

*Just because someone may desire you, it does not mean that he values you.*

for your King. Develop a level of self-control that allows you to take a compliment but still hold true to yourself. I understand that it feels good to hear someone call you beautiful, but have the courage to decline invitations that require your body. Just because someone may desire you, it does not mean that he values you. Regardless of your situation, Queen, you have the power over your temple. Self-worth is determined by what you *think* your worth is. Don't equate self-worth with "likes" on a social media post. Anyone can type something just to appease you for the moment.

We live in a society where abnormal has become normal, and we have become desensitized to many behaviors and practices. Someone has to become an agent of change. I made a decision to not wait on anyone. Therefore, I have become militant in my purpose of ensuring that young Queens all over the world understand that they are more than just their bodies. Many music artists entertain at the expense of young girls not respecting themselves. I don't have to list any songs in particular, but I am sure you can recall several that degrade females. Nothing will change until you do. *If you are not selling yourself as an object, then don't market yourself as one.* Queen, you cannot demand what you do not command. You cannot get respect if you don't first have it for yourself. It is your responsibility to control your body. It cannot be controlled by music, society or your parents. A temple is a special and sacred place. Don't contaminate your temple with foolish acts of lust. Love gives and lust takes. Queen, if you are always giving up your body, this is considered lust rather than love. Getting in and out of bed with different people won't fix anything. It will only make matters worse, both physically and emotionally. Value and cherish your temple, for you only get one. A lack of self-control will leave you out of control. Protect and appreciate your body because it truly is your temple.

*You cannot get respect if you don't first have it for yourself.*

*King Jay*

# "Look at Me"

*A Poem by Brandy Dallas*

Look at me
On December 3, 1983, a baby birthed a baby
My mother was 14 years old
How could she raise me?

Look at me
My first encounter with a demon was at the age of 3
Twenty-four years later
God delivered me

Look at me
Fatherless daughter until the age of 10
But I thank God for my father because
he's a great man

Look at me
Skipping school ... trying to fill voids
Just a lost girl ... chasing after boys

Look at me
Age of 14 ... Sitting in a dark closet crying,
twiddling the tip of a knife in the palm of my hand
Suicide note on the computer screen
Mama, have your man!

Look at me
Pregnant at 15
Lying on an abortion table
Sorry, baby, you gotta go because Mama said so

Look at me
High school dropout ... GED
But, still went to college
What you think of me?

Look at me
Do you see me more clearly?
This is the transparent B
Thought you knew me?
Not nearly

Look at me
Twin pregnancy, what a surprise!
But, to face it ALONE ... what a despise.
And still I RISE!

Look at me
Single mother of two
Never been married, it's true
But, a man does not define me
Let me show you what I can do!

Look at me
One failed relationship after another
Poor choices in men
But only a KING can recognize a QUEEN
So until then, --->"I"<--- will stand

Look at me
Multi-talented
Million-dollar hands
My past does not define me
I Can! I Can! I Can!

Look at me
Oh, B ... I wish I was you.
No ... Honey, be you!
Because to be me,
You would have to go through!

Look at me
No longer smiling through tears
But smiling through Faith
As I know what God has in store for me
Is only to be GREAT

Look at me
My setbacks were my SETUPS
God is taking me to another LEVEL
Power up! Here I go ... new levels, new devils!

Look at me
You see, I'm on a mission
And no matter the obstacles that come
You should NEVER lose sight of your VISION

Look at me
I did not go through this for me
I went though this for you
The very woman who's reading this and thinking
You were the only one going through

Look at me
Before you is a STRONG UNBREAKABLE WOMAN
I've endured!
I've overcome!
And I am still STANDING!

LOOK AT ME!

# The Missing Father

*Dear Queen,*

I hope this letter will lift your spirits and offer you a sense of peace your soul has yet to feel. I pray that what you read encourages you to build from a positive place within. There is a common phrase I often hear in conversations regarding our youth of today: a fatherless child. Although it may be a valid phrase regarding one's situation, it is up to each individual to allow a statement or label to define him or her. According to the U.S. Census, 1 out of 3 children grows up without a father. Although this is heartbreaking, it's a reality for a vast majority of teens growing up today. Reasons for a missing father aren't tied to race. Refusing responsibility is not exclusive to one group or ethnicity. Regardless of your race, social status or background, it all hurts just the same when your father isn't there. It can be very painful and detrimental

*Refusing responsibility is not exclusive to one group or ethnicity.*

to the growth and development of any young girl. Even if you see your father every day, his emotional absence can create the same pain. Queen, I could list statistic after statistic about how many girls will grow up without a father and the negative labels attached to them, but there's no need to be repetitive about this growing epidemic. Doing so will not empower your thinking.

I am reaching out to the young Queen who is missing her father and feels like she is lost or broken. I know that feeling of abandonment and rejection all too well because my father divorced my mother when I was 13. The man that I admired had removed himself from my life. It felt like I was unable to speak because someone had stolen my voice. My father went missing and, therefore, so did I. I missed out on my own life for 15 years. Sometimes, when you go missing in life, very few people come looking for you. I mentally checked out and began to conform to all the labels and negativity that society had predicted I would because I was growing up without a

*You will be the woman you desire to be.*

father. It took a long time, but I eventually learned that no matter what situation surrounded me, it was up to me to reshape it. Queen, if your father walked out of your life, never entered it or comes and goes as he pleases, I am truly sorry. To have something and then lose it can be difficult to grasp. If you lost your voice or mentally checked out as I did, I want to challenge you to check back in to life because you are needed. I couldn't make my father be a part of my life. Some things are out of our control. However, I was in control of myself. Don't let negative labels determine your thinking. Take back your identity and stand tall. You will be the woman you desire to be. Many great women of our time overcame father issues, such as Maya Angelou. It is not your fault. Don't incriminate yourself for something you did not commit. Queen, know that with or without your father, you are *valuable*. When you know that you are valuable, you can then value yourself for more than just your physical attributes. Don't become a statistic just because you were born as one.

*Don't let negative labels determine your thinking. Take back your identity and stand tall.*

When I started mentoring young girls, I was both aware of and prepared for the majority of them having "daddy issues." I was surprised, however, by the different types of issues created by a missing father. One of the young girls, Charity, was living at home with her father, but he was missing emotionally. Whatever his reasons were, he had mentally checked out. His presence, although physical, was invisible because he was absent from his responsibility to love and nourish his daughter. Charity was an attention-seeker. She relished the spotlight and craved acceptance from everyone. When you're not affirmed by your father or male figure, it can create a hole within you that you will try to fill with anything. The affirmation that Charity didn't receive from her father sent her on a boy craze. She went to many lengths for attention and was very promiscuous. One day, Charity agreed to hang out with a boy she really liked. However, without her knowledge, he had also invited several of his friends. While she was engaged in sexual acts with this young man, his friends decided to seize the opportunity. Charity was raped repeatedly by the boys and was threatened to not say a word. She also got pregnant. The kids at school blamed Charity. Her father could not fathom how this had happened on his watch. Regardless of anyone's feelings on the matter, Charity did not deserve the blame. Maybe you can relate to Charity or maybe you know someone who constantly seeks attention because of her missing father. Whether your father is missing physically or emotionally, Queen, you must give attention to yourself before seeking it from someone else. The key to acceptance is accepting who you are

*The key to acceptance is accepting who you are so that you don't worry when others don't accept you.*

so you don't worry when others don't accept you. A missing father is a big problem, but part of the solution is to help you understand who you are as a Queen so that you can handle anything that comes your way.

Loren was another young girl with whom I worked. She never knew her father and so desperately wanted a relationship with him. I believe many young girls have this same desire. There is just something special and unexplainable about a father's love. Loren would constantly talk about how she liked different guys and, most of the time, these guys were several years older. One day, I asked her what she saw in older men. She said they could protect her and make her feel safe. I empathized with her and did not judge her, but I instead posed another question: What are you giving up for this protection? She became silent and her eyes filled with tears. Too many of our young Queens have exchanged their bodies and souls for a false sense of security. If you are reading this letter and you feel like Loren, I want you to know that security should not come at the cost of your body. I know that you want to be accepted and loved. I know that it hurts to not know your father or be able to connect with him. But, Queen, you must still understand your value. Always know that you *do* have a father who will always provide love, security and protection at no cost: God. Only He can give you that, Queen. Hold on to your virtue because it's too precious for just anybody to take. Let God protect it for you until your King comes.

Whether you've encountered a positive or negative experience with men, I am challenging you to not go missing in your life. Who you will or won't become has everything to do with you. A missing father can create a very painful and emotionally crippling situation. I wish all young girls could have their fathers because fathers are needed for so many different reasons. I can blame the economy, education or the justice system, and they all may be at fault. But what difference would it make? Queen, if you excuse yourself from having excuses, you will put every negative statistic about not having a father to shame.

*Keep Ruling*
*King Jay*

# Breaking the Cycle

*Dear Queen,*

I hope this letter touches your soul and helps you realize the changes you must make for the better. At some point we all must answer the call of change or remain the same. The one thing in life that is constant is change, whether we are ready for it or not. As humans, there are two main ways we can form behavioral traits, either through our culture and environment or inherited in our DNA. This inherited behavior is generational and may have been passed down through our bloodlines, whether it be positive or negative. I want to challenge you, Queen, to break the cycle of any negative behaviors or influences that may have attached itself to you. Behaviors that are shown to you and have been prominent in your upbringing will determine what is important to you. For example, if you grew up in an abusive environment, you become more accepting of abuse as an adult. If education was not important in your household, then you may not see the value of continuing your own. Your upbringing shouldn't be an excuse to remain stagnant. I encourage you to break the cycle. Only you possess the power to change what has been. Why *not* you? Many of us continue engaging in bad behaviors because they are all we know. However, it is our responsibility to always seek the better, regardless of whether your parents, family or friends have always done things a certain way. Be different. Finish school. Even if you don't go to college, educate yourself in activities in which you're involved. Knowledge is power, and power gives you the ability to inspire and create change. The hardest thing in life is changing because we all can become victims to our generational ties. Many young Queens fall into the perpetual cycle of doing the same things that they saw their mothers do. It is hard going against the grain. There is nothing easier than just repeating the same old thing. Queen, you are different, and it has nothing to do with thinking you are better than anyone, but I want better for you. You deserve better! You deserve to give yourself a fresh start and do away

*Finish school. Knowledge is power, and power gives you the ability to inspire and create change.*

with the oppression weighing you down in life. Give yourself the opportunity to succeed in life beyond the status quo. Is it hard breaking the cycle? Yes! It is very hard to go against what is inherently present in your bloodline. Sometimes, we develop a mentality that fits our environment and accept the bad versus the good. Some women have convinced themselves they are in good relationships even when they are abused. In their minds, abuse is acceptable because they saw or experienced it and never broke the cycle of being in bad relationships. They have adopted abusive behavior as a part of them. Queen, breaking the cycle goes beyond relationships, social status and even education. Breaking the vicious cycle is changes the influence you have on your future children and other young Queens. Do you want the same negative behavior or characteristic passed down to your children? If your answer is no, then you have a responsibility to break the cycle. You cannot change what you are not willing to confront. The first step in breaking the cycle is acknowledging that things need to change in your life or family.

*You cannot change what you are not willing to confront.*

Queen, there is nothing to feel ashamed of when it comes to desiring a change for the better. I, too, had to break the negative cycle in my life. Some men in my family have a history of spreading their oats across town. I have several close relatives who have kids from multiple women. I decided that was not the path I wanted to take. I don't judge them, but I want to father a child I have with my wife. I had to make a choice and break that cycle. It would have been easy to continue engaging in behaviors associated with what some would call the "family genes." I want to set a new standard because if I don't, my kids will continue down the same path. This letter may be deeply touching to a young Queen who does not have a positive role model. I challenge you to find someone you admire and mirror the positive things he or she does. No one is perfect. Even our role models and people we admire make mistakes, but don't let mistakes alter your path. Break the generational curses that have held you back and set a new standard for yourself. Raise the bar high for yourself, go where there is no path and create your own lane. Be an example for those around you who don't have the courage to change. It is going to take a lot of courage and determination to break any negative, stubborn and generational cycles. Remember, Queen, you have the ability to carry and create life and, therefore, whatever is in you will be passed down. Start now by ridding yourself of bad habits and negative behaviors. No one can change who or what circumstances created them, but we can change what we ourselves create. Queen, no matter what you have seen or heard in your surroundings, you possess the key to lock the door to negative things and open new doors to positive things. You hold the pen to write new values and set new standards by breaking the old cycle. Blaze a new trail, Queen. Break the cycle.

*King Jay*

# What Should You Expect?

*A Poem by Jay Barnett*

What sup, lil mama, I mean dang you a bad chick.

Shawty, tell me if you with it, because if so

We can switch hit with my clique.


Before my man hit, maybe I should let you know
he might be sick

So if you do, you will number your days.

Excuse me! You want some respect?

Girl, look at your dress, all my boy wanted was sex.

What else did you expect?


I get it, you bought into the hype and sold
your soul for a few IG "likes."

You're caught up in bags and shoes,
yet still lonely at night.

Let me guess, you left your man because he
wasn't treating you right?

Now you have soul ties,
knowing you weren't about that life.

Excuse me! You want respect?

Just because you gave up your body,
remember that was your best.

Ooooops ... What else did you expect?


So many women have become thirsty;
they only get left feeling abused and worthless.

Because these dudes could care less.

Despite this, it is hard to teach a woman
how to be a lady,

when she is used to pulling up her dress.

A girl says, I'm dancing for school,

I reply, I wasn't born last night

and I'm most definitely not a fool.

But I don't pass judgment,
so keep doing you, it's cool.

But if you are looking for respect, you might want to
bend down and pick up your rent check.

I don't know what else you expect.


Many can't answer, What is a real man?

I have learned it is hard to build a foundation
where there is no floor plan.

Listen, ladies, I'm just trying to tell you to be
a Queen and take a stand.

Stop saying that you can't when God has given you
the power to say YOU CAN.

Let me get this off my chest. Don't get it twisted.

Because I have to keep it moving on to the next.

I want you to turn down,

before you turn up on a real clown.

He will have you all in his circus turning flips.

Got you thinking you're on a vacation,
because he is a trip.

I hate to be the one to sink your ship

but this is the truth that I spit.

If you don't agree you can have a seat.

Because everyone knows that
where there is no value it's usually sold for free.

But, you want R.E.S.P.E.C.T.

The next time some dude come trying to
fill your head with hype,

let him know you're not about that life.

If he asks you for sex,

tell him you are a Queen and you're
saving your treasure chest.

Listen, life is more than drama and
keeping up with mess.

You are not cursed,

Because God called you blessed.

So get focused and stop retaking the same old test.

And tell these dudes you don't have time to stress

because you need your beauty rest.

Most of all, every Queen is deserving of
her self-respect.

And that is what you should EXPECT.

# No Matter What

Torn between what you see and what you hear

has given you a misconception of a blurred line
that is not yet clear

Your thoughts travel afar, but your pain remains near

Many lonely nights of confusion interrupt your sleep
because your eyes drown in tears

You cannot change what you have seen,

but that does not change that you are a QUEEN.


It puzzles me why sometimes the good ones
have it so hard,

But life goes on, it's too late to fold your hand and
throw in your cards.

You were left with broken promises and
a broken heart,

I understand that it is difficult to have respect for
those who didn't do their part

Don't give up, get your education because the
baddest chick is so very smart.

No matter what you may have seen

It doesn't matter because you are a QUEEN.


Comparison is an act of violence

Sometimes you have to speak up,
otherwise you will be consumed by your own silence

Give attention to details, one of the greatest
combinations is education and common sense

Because time wasted is time that was freely spent.

Always surround yourself with people
who support you and your dreams

Because Queens always support other Queens


Your beauty goes far beyond the surface of your skin

This world is full of all types of people,
not everyone was meant to be thin.

That does not mean you have to have a certain figure

When you are comfortable with yourself,
that will make others reconsider

What is sad? The most sought-out profession is
becoming a stripper

Now so many of our young princesses
fall for these tricksters

No matter what you have heard or seen

You cannot change that you are a QUEEN

I know it hurts to not have a father,
but don't keep lying in your pain

Life is full of uncertainties, just like a meteorologist
predicts sunshine then it rains

But there is nothing worse than remembering
something that you can't change

No matter what, it is up to you to evolve
into a great WOMAN

Invest in yourself and play the cards you
have in your hand

No matter what you have heard or seen

You cannot change that you are a QUEEN


It is your responsibility to make sure you are whole

Give no man your body if he is not ready to be
responsible for your soul

Its hard to break the behaviors of what we have seen,
but you have to reshape that mold

Stay in your lane and remain focused on your goals.

No matter what you have heard or seen

You cannot change that you are a QUEEN

# Forgive

*Dear Queen,*

I hope this letter encourages you to let go of any negative feelings you have against someone who has wronged you. I am going to challenge you to forgive and move on. Forgiveness is hard for many of us, because we all feel anger and hurt when it comes to an injustice. I want to address the young Queen who is still clinging to the nightmares, bad memories, pain and hurt that seemingly won't go away. I want to address the young Queen who said she would never forgive and she definitely won't forget. I want to address the young Queen who is seeking revenge and has let bitterness become her navigation system. Many of us have used pain to empower our drive in life, but that source of fuel always runs out. You can only drive so far using the same fuel before you are stranded on the side of the road. I don't want to be insensitive to any negative or traumatic event that may have taken place in your life, but I want you to know that you possess the power to free yourself from the pain it caused. Forgetting what was done will not be easy, but you can't move forward while holding grudges. Not forgiving can be like cancer—if it is not taken care of early, it can be detrimental. The longer you hold it in your heart, the longer it will take you to heal. Forgiving is all about your freedom, Queen. The sooner you move forward, the better it is for your soul. Bitterness as an adult usually comes from not forgiving an act that occurred when you were young. It will be hard for your future to breathe if you continue drowning it with your past. Don't incarcerate yourself because of something that you couldn't control. We don't have the power to control what people do to us. Even if you were violated by a close family member or you have hatred toward your parents, the only things we can control are how we treat people and how we respond after being wronged. No matter the situation, forgiving someone is about *your* freedom. I was 13 when my parents divorced, and I hated and resented my father for more than 15 years of my life. I am now 32. I lived in a jail of bitterness for all those years and, come to find out, I held the

*It will be hard for your future to breathe if you continue drowning it with your past.*

key to free myself all along. I did not want to forgive my dad for walking out on my mother, his wife of 15 years with 3 children. I used all the hurt and pain as fuel to play football. When football ended, that fuel was no longer effective. This took me to a place of depression and suicide because I had nothing else to start my engine. I had always boasted about how I would never forgive my dad, but I was only hurting myself. My dad moved on and I was still holding on, missing out on my future. My life was going nowhere. I was always angry at the world. I was negative and people did not want to be around me. Bitterness is a bad aroma that stinks up any room quickly. If we have hatred, bitterness and anger, they always manage to be present toward others. They also stunt your growth as a young Queen and as a human being.

One day, I wrote my dad a letter telling him that I forgave him and that I just wanted him to know it. Afterward, I felt like I had lost 100 pounds. I had carried all of that weight and was miserable in life. Will I ever forget what happened to my parents? No. But the pain is not there anymore. Just like a scar from an accident, it hurts at first and for a while after but, over time, it heals.

*Don't hold your future captive because of your past.*

The scar remains, but the pain doesn't. Some say time heals all wounds, but I say only God can heal your wounds at any time. The key is that we must be willing to forgive and move on. We go to God all the time about our mistakes and sins after we mess up. We ask his forgiveness for acts we knew were wrong as we were committing them. We all have a little hypocrisy in us. We only forgive when it is convenient for us. Queen, I don't know what has transpired in your life, but I know this: You *can* forgive and move forward. Don't hold your future captive because of your past. You may have experienced devastating pain but you must forgive so you can blossom into the Queen you were born to be. Move forward in life and embrace the present. Queen, don't self-destruct because you are unforgiving toward a person who broke your heart or promise. This person may have broken your heart for the moment, but he or she didn't ultimately break you. Many young Queens lose control because of bitterness, but don't ruin your kingdom because of someone else's wrongdoing. Whoever hurt you had a responsibility and should be held accountable, but you have a bigger responsibility. You are responsible for *you*. Always take care of yourself. Don't let anyone hold you hostage because of what he or she did. You have the power to free yourself. Queen, you are too valuable to let others' actions destroy your future. I wish I could tell you that no one will ever disappoint or take advantage of you. I wish I could tell you that you can trust all family members. I wish I could say this world has nothing but good people. Unfortunately, I would be telling you lies and setting you up for failure. This is life and it is full of unexpected events. I will tell you that your future is waiting on you to forgive your past and everyone in it. I will tell you that you don't have to use anger as fuel. You can be driven by the mere fact that you are a Queen. Accept what is, let go of what was and have faith in what will be. No matter your age or where you are in life, forgive and move forward. Free yourself, Queen, and rule your kingdom.

*King Jay*

# Conclusion

There exist a plethora of factors that continuously blind the eyes of our young Queens from seeing their worth. Society constantly fluctuates its views and morals to match our growing appetite for instant gratification. This epidemic brings suffering upon many young girls, regardless of their backgrounds, experiences or environments. Society views women as objects, and the fault lies with us for allowing this type of mentality to ensue. As an uncle, brother and future father, I am making it my business and my mission to mentor as many young Queens as possible. I wholeheartedly believe that it is only when men find their rightful place, become more involved and stop being passive that a change will begin to unfold in the minds of our Queens. There are many young Queens who are lost and looking for love in all the wrong places simply because they haven't received the proper care and guidance in seeing their value. Just one positive word can alter the trajectory of someone's path. Positivity is a necessary tool that bestows our Queens with the confidence to take a stand and set their standards high. Too many young women are negotiating their value, thus leading to dreams deferred, lives lost and babies born into a perpetual cycle of bad decision-making. I cannot change every young girl's path, but I know I can create and influence positive change for many Queens. I refuse to let negative music, social media and other outlets dictate how my nieces view themselves. The amazing thing about being a mentor is having the ability to redirect the path of an individual willing to change. I pray that every young Queen who read this book will be able to both identify her worth and comprehend it beyond her physical capabilities. I challenge females of all ages to uplift each other with love and treat one another as sisters. Jealousy is an ugly disease that serves to only destroy the jealous person at the end. Queens build Queens. They share their stories not to impress but rather to encourage one another to improve. Remove the barriers of bitterness and open your heart to receive love from other Queens. Cut out the drama and get rid of the antics that portray women as catty creatures. Queen, you have a huge responsibility to rule your body, as well as your mind. Don't allow filthy gossip to poison your kingdom with he-says-she-says games. If you don't have anything royal to say, don't bother to contribute your thoughts aloud. Monitor your behavior and always carry yourself as if someone is watching. You may be the only example for another young Queen. Walk with integrity and never compromise your standards for a temporary feeling that may cause you permanent pain. Learn how to take a compliment and pass it along. Be the kind of friend who does not seek benefits. When your character commands respect, you will never have to demand respect. I cannot emphasize this enough, Queen: Love you, love you, love you. No one but God will love you better than you love yourself. Don't expect people to do what you don't do. People will treat you how you treat yourself. Walk like a Queen, talk like a Queen, smile like a Queen, encourage like a Queen, empower like a Queen and love like a Queen. I hope these letters have touched the depth of your soul. I hope they have brought light into the darkness that filled your heart. Queen, when you truly come to know who you are, you will never have to ask anyone to define you. It is not what they call you but what you answer to. Always remember, you are a QUEEN. Never remove your crown.

*Keep Ruling Your Kingdom (Mind, Body and Soul)*
*King Jay*

To redefine your kingdom and claim your throne, start by changing your language...

Seven-Day Affirmations

## Monday

Today I will begin my week with words that will shape the kingdom of my mind. I am ready to accept the responsibility of ruling my territory. I will build up others around me by using uplifting words to build their kingdoms. I am a Queen.

## Tuesday

Today I will step out of my comfort zone and encourage another Queen to dream outside of her situation and see beyond the negative barriers that are holding her hostage. I will build a Queen today.

## Wednesday

Today I will find the positive energy to push beyond my fatigue. I will be a light to those around me. I will embody the character of a Queen.

## Thursday

Today I will pray for those who have been hurt, abused or violated. I will donate my energy toward those who need restoration. Today I will restore another Queen.

## Friday

Today I will celebrate the achievement of another week of accomplishments and disappointments. No matter what has happened, I will reflect on the positive and learn from the negative.

## Saturday

Today I will enjoy a day of relaxation and celebrate the Queen I am. I will discover the adventures of life. I will enjoy a day of great conversations and fellowship. Today I will enjoy being a Queen.

## Sunday

Today I will be grateful for the day of the sabbath. I will pour God's word into my soul. I will refuel and realign myself to the purpose of God, for my kingdom needs His guidance. I will prepare my mind, body and soul for another week in my kingdom. My week will be a royal one because I am a Queen. I declare the kingdom I desire to live in.

# Acknowledgments

I am blessed to be able to encourage and inspire young people all over the world with my message. I am grateful to God, who has given me such an awesome purpose to fulfill. I want to thank my family for their continued support and prayers. I love each of you. This book was inspired by the young girls that were a part of the WE (Women of Excellence) project.

# About the Author

Jay Barnett was raised down in the Delta in a small Mississippi town called Gunnison. He graduated from Tarleton State University with a Bachelor of Science degree. Long after his pursuit in the NFL, Jay turned to his childhood gift, speaking to and empowering teens. Jay's vision has become a newfound message for many teens and adults. The I AM A KING & I AM A QUEEN movement has taken the community by storm.

Jay's passion is undeniably his greatest asset. He began a 5-week self-development program called The ME Project, which is geared toward teen boys and girls in the Houston, Texas, area where he now resides. Jay's vision is to reach the world with his message of empowering teens to be Kings and Queens and never servants to anything or anyone but God.

80793331R00053

Made in the USA
San Bernardino, CA
01 July 2018